5 EASY STEPS TO READING

SHIRLEY GAITHER & MARY ANN MOON

5 Steps to Easy Reading by Shirley Gaither with Mary Ann Moon

Self-Published by Shirley Gaither

© 2017 Shirley Gaither

ISBN: 978-1-952725-64-7

Original Cover by Designrr, recreated for this edition by Melissa Williams Design

About Shirley Gaither

Shirley Gaither has taught students to read for 27 years. She has used this particular program for 14 years with great success. Ninety-five percent of the students she teaches obtain benchmark on district kindergarten and first grade tests. She has experience teaching struggling and gifted students. She maintains a high level of trust in educating students. At the present time she is a member of the teaching staff in Canyons School District in the state of Utah.

About Mary Ann Moon

Mary Ann Moon has just recently retired from teaching. She taught kindergarten for 27 years in three different school districts. She taught children on many different levels and has seen all of them have success. She has taught reading using many different methods and feel her experience has helped her teach the best parts of all the different programs. Her greatest joy and her greatest accomplishment was watching young children learn to read and learn to love it.

Table Of Contents

Beginning Reading

I well remember my delight when first The meaning of a printed sentence burst Upon me; I had vaguely sensed a link Between the symbols reproduced in ink And what was read to me, but had not found The kinship of the letters and the sound. Then suddenly at once I understood that there Incorporated in these symbols lay The language I was speaking every day.

- Anonymous

Why I Wrote This Book

It is so exciting to write a book that will make a positive difference in the lives of so many children.

As educators and parents it is a great privilege to stimulate students with a desire to learn while building confidence and trust. The manner in which we interact with children, stimulate their environment, and curriculum affects how motivated and successful they will become.

Children learn to read by acquiring vocabulary, phonetic, and phonemic skills. They learn to hear syllables, individual sounds in words, and rhyming words. It is important that children learn these skills at an early age and are monitored with blending consonants and vowels in order to create words.

Reading empowers students. Reading enables them to use that power to take care of their own lives and learning. The 5 steps to reading involve children in the reading process with activities that will stimulate their thinking and cognitive abilities.

Initial reading instruction relies on specific skills. Most reading programs acquaint teachers and parents with phonetic and phonemic awareness and are a great support.

This book will guide children in preschool through first grade the knowledge and skills needed to learn to read and write with the correct handwriting techniques. These skills have logic, order, and meaning which will help children read independently. Children will be begin applying sounds with basic consonants and vowels which will be blended into words within the first few weeks of the program. Children find it difficult to recognize the sounds of the entire alphabet at once, so we start teaching them to recognize and associate just a few sounds the first few weeks of this program.

Understanding how to associate a few letters and sounds helps the children hear and distinguish separate sounds in words. Children begin this association by using their senses in association to the sounds of the alphabet.

It is also vitally important that children have multiple opportunities to memorize and understand the use of sight words in the reading process. These are key words that typically cannot be sounded out and must simply be memorized. In the first week of this program one to two sight words are introduced and 2-3 sight words are added each consecutive week. We include activities for teachers and parents to practice sight word (see step #4).

The last step relies on parents to help their children learn. Success in reading recognizes parents as the key element for successful readers. Positive involvement with parents and children is key in learning to read.

In this program an assortment of motivational and instructional hands on letter-sound games, rhymes, flash cards, and bingo games will facilitate school and in home learning.

The 5 steps to read include using, all our senses, phonetic and phonemic blending, segmentation, sight words and parent participation.

With these skills a child can read in 90 days.

Parent Testimonials

The following parent comments explain the incredible results at the end of the year.

I really like the method taught to learn how to read. Thanks to this method my children know how to read better, can learn words faster, and also understand what they are learning as well. - DMA

We have had 3 children who have all gone through this program. All 3 of them knew how to read by the end of their kindergarten year. We believe that having mastered the skill of reading at such early age has helped them immensely in their schooling. Each child reads at least one to two grade levels above the grade they are currently in. This helps them excel in other areas. They all enjoy reading and doing of their own free will. The reading program is wonderful and easy for the children to learn. It is a positive learning tool and helps build the child's self-esteem as they realize they can read. - Peter and Karen Kuhn

The reading program introduced to our daughter Savanna stimulated her interest to read. The homework for practicing reading was fun and involved by wife and myself in helping our daughter learn. The weekly challenges were fun for our daughter, who learned to read easily. Thank you - Daniel C.

This reading system is going to brighten the next generation. It is wonderful - Amy Gutierrez

I have 3 daughters and unfortunately my first daughter didn't have this program. Fortunately, my second daughter did have this program. It is an excellent program that enabled my second daughter to read ahead of her peers. Thank you. - Lewis Moore

I have loved this reading program. My daughter went from not being able to put two sounds together to reading on a first grade level. What's more important is she loves to read, and I feel much is due to this reading program. It puts confidence into the children and raises the expectations so they reach it. I wish so much my older son could have been involved in the program. - Mrs. Anita Cripps

This reading program is wonderful! My daughter was reading first and second grade books when she was only 5 years old! She learned to read so fast it seemed like she learned to read overnight! I just think this reading program is great! - Jennifer Griffiths

This reading program is exceptional. My son loves to read and loves to sow other's that he can read first and second grade reading level books. Developing this skill this young is a good self-motivator and self-esteem builder. - Elizabeth Cracroft

Step One - Using Our Senses

Introduction

Reading is built upon a foundation of language skills children have learned since birth. Most children develop skills through different activities through their environment, and home, and school. At three years of age they like to listen to stories. As they grow older children love to print letters, listen to songs, and play games.

As children begin school, parents and family members have ambitious expectations. These expectations include literacy, academic competence, social and emotional independence. As parents and teachers we need to meet these expectations.

A child starts early to discover the world around them through their senses. The world becomes clear to them through taste, touch, smell, hearing, and seeing.

As children develop, they use their senses automatically; however, at times they aren't aware of a particular sense in a situation. They are not aware of the information that is gathered. If children learn by using as many of the 5 senses as possible the information they learn will be retained and learned easily.

This section describes some sensory activities to work with to enhance the acquisition of reading.

SMELL

MATERIALS: Gather the following items and show them to students: onion, lemon, lotion, soap, vinegar, etc.

PROCEDURE: Cover a child's eyes with a blindfold. The child then picks up one item at a time, smells it and identifies the object and says the first sound of the object. This activity can be expanded with different foods like oranges, peanut butter, garlic or cinnamon. Place the food in containers covered with foil. Number the containers and ask the children to guess what they think is in each container by smelling it.

DISCUSSION: Explain that each word begins with an initial sound. When this sound is isolated it helps us to understand and read by listening, seeing, and smelling the beginning sound of the object. By combining the first sound of the object with the sense of smell a child can learn the sound of the letter much quicker while retaining and understanding this knowledge.

C   G   O   P

TOUCH

ACTIVITY 1:

MATERIALS: Use a small box or fabric bag and place some small items in it. Ask the children to guess what each item is by the sense of touch. Then ask them what the first sound of the object is. Items could include socks, pencil, tissue paper, cotton ball, eraser, coins, etc.

ACTIVITY 2: Walking and touching. Go on a walk and look for things with different textures. Some examples could include: rocks, leaves, petals, sticks, pine cones, etc. Have the children bring the items inside, have each child tell the name of the item collected and the beginning sound of that item.

C   P   S   R

TASTE

ACTIVITY 1

TASTING THE ALPHABET MATERIALS: A variety of foods that have the same beginning sound as the letter or letters being focused on during the week or a given period of time. Select foods that are salty, sweet, bitter, spicy, bland, etc. Discuss the tastes of the foods. State that a lemon is sour, some crackers are salty, and candy is sweet.

apple   banana   candy   doughnut   Easter candy   fries

grapes   jam   kiwi   licorice   m&m's   nuts   orange   pie

quinoa   raisins   strawberry   tater tots   ugli fruit

vegetables   watermelon   xigua   yucca root   zucchini

A   N   Q   Z

5 Easy Steps to Reading by Shirley Gaither

Activities to Engage the Senses

SIGHT:

Have children write the letter of the alphabet they are working on. Write both capital and lower case letters. Write the letter 8-10 times each. Show the children a picture that begins with the same letter and sound they are writing.

TOUCH:

Using cookie cutters of the letters of the alphabet, cut the letters out of playdough. Sponge paint the letter of the alphabet the children are working on. Glue a letter on a piece of paper, have the children cover the letter with various items. These could include cotton balls, q-tips, glitter, sequins, beans, etc. Cut letters out of wallpaper, felt, cardboard, sponges, etc.

TASTE:

Make a fruit salad. Assign each child a letter of the alphabet and have them bring a fruit that begins with that letter. Cut up the fruit and enjoy your fruit salad. If it is around Thanksgiving time, have each child draw a letter out of a box. Bring an item that begins with that letter to the feast.

HEARING:

While the children are writing a letter have the child say the sound of the letter aloud. Have the children write stories sounding out the letters as they are written. Music to sing that pronounce the letters and sounds.

SMELL:

Write the letters with fingernail polish Write the letters with milk, and make the letters appear by rubbing lemon juice over them.

Step Two - Phonemic Awareness

Introduction

Most children can be able to read simple and nonsense words in three or four weeks. When they can recognize and identify the sound of 10 letters including vowels children can blend them to make words. Parents and teachers are encouraged to also teach vocabulary words with a lot of repetition to use many new words spontaneously.

Children who have a good phonemic awareness can also write words with inventive spelling, where they write according to the sounds they hear in words.

When children are aware and can produce sounds of letters in their environment, pick 3-4 letters of the alphabet (m,s,a,t) and teach children the sounds of these letters. Teach the sounds one letter at a time, teaching no more than 2 sounds in a week.

When the children can discriminate and identify the sounds blend the sounds together (see step 3). Always teach the sound and name of the letter together in order to facilitate the child being able to read words in 3-4 weeks.

The ability to read quickly and understand and know letters and sounds is extremely effective as parents and teachers work together. In the beginning of this process children will focus on learning 10 letters and sounds including vowels. Later they will learn the skills of phonemic segmentation and auditory blending. Along with these letters, sounds, blending, and segmentation it is important to add game and activities that facilitate the learning process.

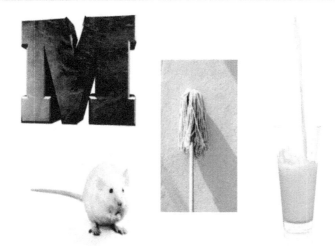

LETTER/SOUND ACTIVITIES WITH /Mm/

1. Marching holding the letter Mm repeating the sound aloud over and over again while marching.

2. Hide some objects that begin with the sound of m. Have the children find the item.

3. Have children say the letter/sound and an action in which they make the letter m with their arms of legs.

4. Show children items that begin with the letter m ie.(mouse, mirror, mop, mitten, milk carton, moon, magnet, etc). Hold up each item and say the names of each item and the beginning sound. As each object is named put them in a pillowcase or paper sack.

5. Letter formation. Direct children in writing capital and lowercase m using a document camera.

6. Ask children to find items in the room that begin with the letter m. &. Discover and cut out pictures in magazines or draw pictures that begin with the letter m.

LETTER/SOUND ACTIVITIES WITH /Ss/

1. Read and have children repeat a short tongue twister that begins with s and repeat it several times. Example: Sammy sells sea shells by the sea shore. See how fast they can say it.

2. Show real items: sock, soap, salt, sand, sauce, scarf, etc. that begin with s. Children repeat the names and sounds of each item.

3. Sort pictures that begin with /s/.

4. Use playdough and have the children make the letter /s/.

5. With sidewalk chalk make /s/ on the playground and sidewalk.

6. Student lay on the floor and form /s/ with their body.

7. Write capital and lowercase /s/.

8. Create letter journals where children write the letter and words that begin with the letter.

9. Sort and group items that begin with /m/ /s/.

LETTER/SOUND ACTIVITIES WITH /Pp/

1. Read stories where /p/ is used frequently and emphasized (scholastic has a set of alphabet books).

2. Gather stuffed objects with the initial sound of /p/ such as: pig, puppets, pillow, pumpkin, and other various items that begin with /p/: paint, peanuts, plastic plates, pencils, etc.

3. Find or prepare flashcards of the letters /m/ /p/ /s/. Sort these flashcards as children name the picture on the flashcards and repeat the initial sound.

4. Write capital and lowercase /p/.

5. Draw pictures and write words in journals of words that begin with /p/.

LETTER/SOUND ACTIVITIES WITH /Ff/

1. Painting and writing the word "fish."

2. Have items such as: fork, fan, feather, five, four, fish, football, etc. Put the items in a pillowcase or paper sack. Blindfold one child at a time and have them describe the feel of the item as it is pulled out of the pillowcase or sack. Also have the child say the name of the item and the beginning sound.

3. Divide children into groups of 5. Assign each group a specific letter. Each group will cut and paste pictures from magazines that begin with their assigned letter. And the end children will display their work on the wall.

4. Have children sit in a circle and put the letters /m/ /s/ /p/ /f/ on the floor in front of them. Children throw bean bags on the letters and say the name of the letter and the corresponding sound.

5. Write capital and lowercase f.

6. Journal writing and drawing of words that begin with f.

7. Give each child a flashcard with the letter /m/ /s/ /p/ /f/ as the teacher or parent says a word that begins with one the sounds the child holds up the card of the matching sound.

LETTER/SOUND ACTIVITIES WITH /Tt/

1. Have students bring to class or find at home small items that begin with /t/: ticket, tie, toothbrush, tennis ball, teaspoon, token, toilet paper, trash bag, timer, etc. Put all the items on a table or the floor. Have children pick an item, describe it, and say the name and sound of the beginning sound.

2. Have children draw a few of the above items and display them.

3. Find and sort different items from the classroom or home that start with /m/ /s/ /p/ /f/ /t/. 4. Put children in small groups and match pictures to the letters mentioned above.

LETTER/SOUND ACTIVITIES WITH /Hh/

1. Horse Racing Game: Show the children how to gallop like a horse and gallop inside or outside for a few minutes. As the children gallop have them imitate the sound "huh huh huh.

2. Show the children different pictures with different beginning sounds. Every time the picture begins with the "huh" sound or letter /Hh/ have the children stand up.

3. Write capital and lowercase /Hh/.

4. Continue writing and drawing in journals words and pictures that begin with the letter /Hh/.

LETTER/SOUND ACTIVITIES WITH THE SHORT VOWEL /Aa/

1. Write the letter Aa in sand, whip cream, pudding, paint, etc.

2. Read short stories to the children and every time they hear the short sound of /a clap their hands.

3. Write capital and lowercase /Aa/.

4. Pass out a card for each letter of the alphabet you have learned so far. Have th children put the letters face up on their desk or rug. The adult says aloud a word tha begins with a sound/letter the child knows. The child holds up the correspondin card of the beginning sound of the word.

LETTER/SOUND ACTIVITES WITH LETTERS /Bb/ /Cc/ /Oo/

1. Mix and match all the afore mentioned activities and repeat with the name and sounds of /b/ /c/ /o/. Teach these letters separately.

2. Have students sit in a circle and take turns throwing a bean bag on picture cards on the rug that begin with the above letters. Teach letters separately.

3. Prepare pictures of students on a flashcard. Have the students match the beginning sound and letter to only the letters and sounds we have learned thus far.

4. Have children play the beginning card game for each letter one at a time that is mentioned above #4.

Step Three - Blending Sounds

Introduction

Blending individual sounds to make words is easy if done the correct way. This skill will be very useful as students learn to match sounds to symbols and decode words.

Studies of linguistics and cognitive psychologists refer to the idea that young children need to pay attention to individual sounds and how they are formed. Children also need to be aware of sound patterns, rhymes, and alliteration. A child's ability to perform phonemic segmentation and auditory blending are inherent of the child's reading achievement. Psycholinguistics emphasize that this is more important than vocabulary, cognitive abilities, and environment.

When children are taught to hear individual sound is words they are able to decode and read them with ease. An adult can make these skills an active hands on experience. That last pages of this chapter will explain this phenomenon.

When the children are able to recognize and identify two consonants and a vowel they are ready to blend and segment CVC words (consonant-vowel-consonant).

The adult will hold up a card with #1 for the first sound #2 for the second sound, and #3 for the third sound.

The procedure begins like this:

*Show a few pictures ie. mat, hat, bat, cat

*Explain to the children that they are going to segment the names of a few pictures.

Activity #1

Show the items one at a time. Hold up number cards or you can also use flyswatters with the numbers 1, 2, 3 on them. When using the flyswatters you will also need the letters of the word your segmenting on them. Show the children a picture and have them tell you the first, second, and third sound or the word and hold up the corresponding flyswatters. Do this with the as many CVC words as possible.

MAT   CAT

BAT   HAT

This can also be done by holding up fingers representing the sounds of the words being segmented.

Activity #2

Demonstrate to the children how to say each sound by holding up a number stick.

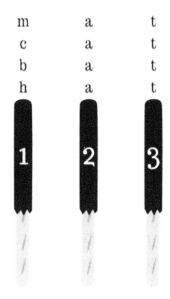

Show children how to push up letters using the following card. Do this activity of segmenting every time a new consonant letter or vowel is introduced.

top
mop
pot

Activity #3

Have children make new words every time a new consonant or vowel is introduced. Change the beginning, middle, and ending sounds to make new words.

dot	cot
pet	net
set	get
kit	fit
lap	cap

Make a set of flash cards for each child containing each letter of the alphabet or use the ones in the activities in the back of this book. When a new letter is introduced, hand out just that letter to the child. When 2 letters and a vowel are introduced and passed out have the children make words. The words can be real or nonsense words. Do this with every letter that is introduced until the child has a complete set of the alphabet. You can also download this set of flashcards!

Activity #4

Practice making and reading words with the cards. Use the following list of words for homework.

dim win fit rid lip

pet wet net set let jet
bed fed wed web hen
met bet get leg pen
hog dog sob dot not
got log pop log sop
cop job lot top hot

bun fun sun run pun
nut hut mut put rut
jud rud cud dud mud

Use words in short sentences so children connect the meaning of the word to the picture. Have some objects or pictures scattered around the room of the sample words. Then ask the children a question: Where is the mat? The children then answer in complete sentences: The mat is on the table.

Practicing Oral Blending

Oral blending is an activity that helps students understand how spoken words are smaller units of sounds and word parts. The most effective and simplest way to blend words is to say the first sound and second sound separately. Then blend and hold those two sounds while saying the last sound. For instance the word "bam" a child would say 'bu" then short sound of /a/. Pause and blend those two sounds saying "baa" holding out the last sound then drop in the /m/ sound ie. bu..aa..blend and hold baa..m.

EXAMPLE:

Pod   pu..o..blend and hold po..d
Pop   pu..o..blend and hold po..p
Rag   er..aa..blend and hold ra..g
Mat mm..aa..blend and hold ma..t
Back   bu..aa..blend and hold ba..k
Mad   mm..aa..blend and hold ma..d
Bin   bu..i..blend and hold bi..n
Tab   tu..aa blend and hold ta..b

SEGMENTATION (Breaking down words into parts or syllables)

SYLLABICATION

Syllabication is also a good way to break down words. This way words can be blended in parts of syllables.

En......ter   rock.....et
Pow.....der   post....er
Sis.....ter   be.....tween
Ta.....ble   pil.....low

Step Four - Using High Frequency Words

Introduction

The reading process also involves high frequency words, often called sight words. These are words that usually cannot be sounded out or blended. They just need to be memorized. Most of these words do not follow the rules for blending or sound letter correspondence. This word recognition is vital in gaining reading fluency. When sight words are used in meaningful context, fluency and comprehension are improved.

where this is no it yes me for go my what have do is she look can to the not are at you he here and we see I has too said up like have good big home was from play one two three four five six seven eight nine ten orange yellow red green blue purple

Children should learn 2-3 sight words per week. These words appear frequently in sentences and texts. Children should memorize these and apply them to reading and writing activities. Children need many opportunities to experience, manipulate, and understand each word.

The adult will decide which sight words to memorize each week depending on reading material and activities being taught. Sight word activities can be done as a whole class activity, small group, or independent activity. Select games where children are involved in kinesthetic, visual, and auditory learning style.

Activity

The following activities facilitate the understanding and memorization of sight words.
1. At the beginning of the week introduce the sight words being studied. As a whole group say the words separately and then as a chant. When additional sight words are added to the curriculum, review the previous sight words also, until 5-7 sight words are reviewed in a week.

The **is** _____

1. Prepare or buy a memory game for the sight words your child knows. Explain how to play the game and use the game as an independent activity.

2. Demonstrate sight words being used in a sentence and have your child read the sentence with you and independently.

3. Have your child choose a sight word from a stack of cards. Give your child a beanbag in which they will throw on a sight word say the word and use it in a sentence.

4. Write 20 sight words on the surface of a large ball. Roll the ball to your child and have them say a word on the ball that is facing them. Take turns rolling the ball until all words are said.

5. Pick a sight word card from a stack of cards. After your child picks the card they spell it out with magnetic letters.

I have a big

6. Make a sight word book for your child to read to you.

7. Have your child copy a sight word from the board on a piece of paper. Sprinkle glue and glitter on the letters of the word.

8. When your child writes stories have them use 2-4 sight words.

9. Write the words on cards and put them on the wall under the alphabet letter in which the word begins. This will make a word wall for your child to refer to as they write sentences and stories.

10. Give your child sponges or stamps and have them stamp or sponge paint the sight words from a word card.

11. Make a center by the word wall. Have your child write notes to their friend. Also have a list of children's names easily accessible. Teach them how to use the words "to" and "from" in their notes.

12. Point to words on the wall and have children say the words pointed as they leave the house.

Parents As Partners

Introduction

When parents are involved in the learning process, the children are positively affected. Working with children for more than 25 years has proven to me that children where the parents actively support them at home help children succeed. Parents give their children a tremendous advantage by reading to them, helping with homework, communication with their teachers, etc. Parents helping their children at home is especially important in reading. Parents help by talking, listening, and reading with their child every day.

There are a few success factors that when parents are involved in the learning process. Parents can be involved in the classroom by:

1. Creating and preparing projects for the class.
2. Another factor is reading skills are reinforced at home.
3. Helping in the classroom with phonetic and phoneme activities.
4. Going on fieldtrips
5. Helping with class projects
6. Participate in reading and game activities.
7. Help struggling students in reading and writing skills.
8. Read stories to the students.

An important factor in any reading program is the participation of well-informed parents. It is recommended that parents and teachers have one on one meetings to discuss goals, share research, see their child's work samples (pictures, journals, writing, etc.). It is important to read and examine weekly or monthly letters sent home. That way parents are informed of what is being taught in the classroom, and reinforce the skills at home.

Parent volunteers are wonderful allies in helping children practice skills, making and gathering resources, and helping with small group instruction.

What Parents Can Do

Read the school notes every day.

Teach your child how to acquire good study habits by choosing a place that is comfortable and free from distractions.

Let the child do the work themselves.

Praise all efforts.

Keep in touch with the teacher by notes, phone calls, and emails.

Turn off the TV and other electronics.

Provide supplies: pencils, eraser, markers, scissors, glue, etc.

Encourage children to put all their supplies in one place every day.

Read aloud to your children so they can develop a sense of language structure, vocabulary, and the concept of print.

Homework

Doing homework with your child keeps the parent aware of what expected of the child and how they are doing.

Make homework fun for the young child. Play games either physical or on the computer, ipad, etc. If you as a parent are not available, siblings and grandparents can always help.

Homework is a time when the parent can help a struggling child master a certain concept. For instance, if the child is not grasping the sound of a certain letter, a parents help can be extremely beneficial.

According to Rhoda McShane Becker children with high test scores have parents that:

1. Have high expectations for their children
2. Respond to and interact with their children frequently
3. See themselves as teachers

Teachers and parents that help with homework thrive by making sure both parties understand their roles and responsibilities.

Learning occurs frequently when it is goal directed and clear as to what needs to be accomplished.

In each step in this book, parents can find great ideas to make homework fun and enjoyable for children. Parents, siblings, and grandparents, can participate in the learning activities.

A or E in the Middle

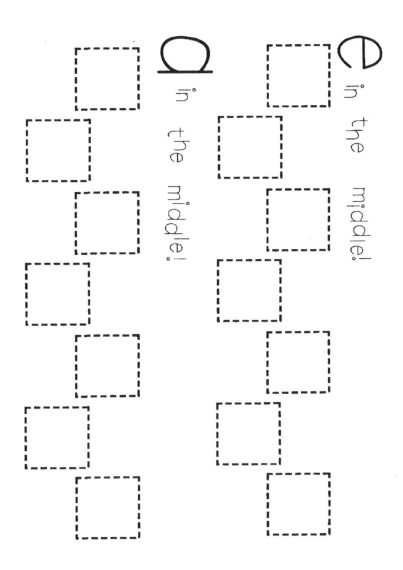

A Worksheet - Big

Cut out the pictures on the Aa page in the dotted lines and glue all the pictures that start with the Aa sound on the apple page.

Aa

A-B Pictures

A-D Alphabet Cards

A or E Middle Pictures

a or e middle pictures

A Writing

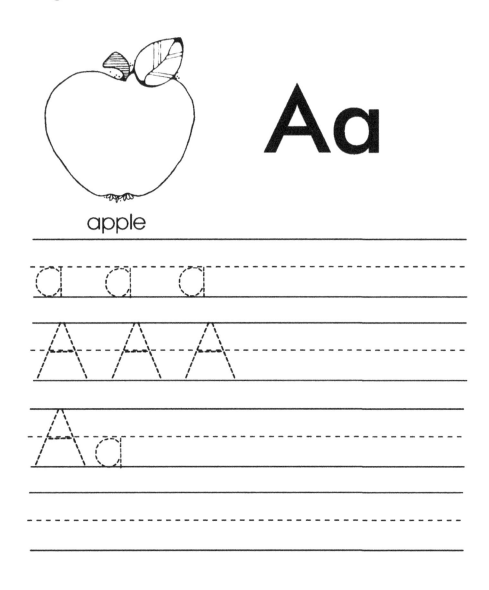

apple

B Worksheet Big

Cut out the pictures on the Bb page in the dotted lines and glue all the pictures that start with the Bb sound on the bear page.

B Writing

bear

Bb

C Worksheet Big

Cut out the pictures on the Cc page in the dotted lines and glue all the pictures that start with the Cc sound on the cat page.

C Writing

cat

Cc

C-D Pictures

D Worksheet Big

Cut out the pictures on the Dd page in the dotted lines and glue all the pictures that start with the Dd sound on the dog page.

D Writing

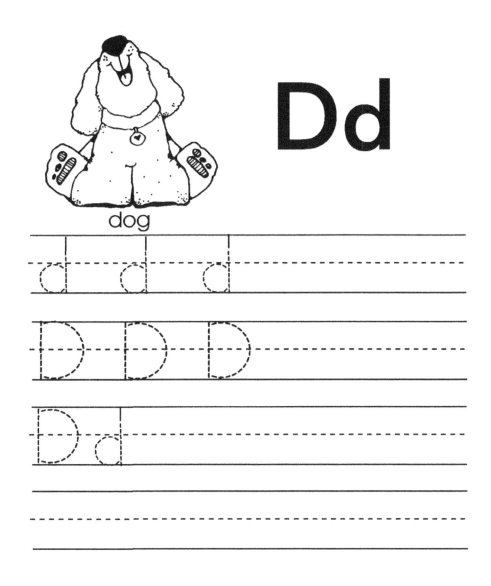

dog

Dd

E Worksheet Big

Ee

Cut out the "Ee" pictures on the other page. Glue the pictures that start with the Ee sound on this page.

E Writing

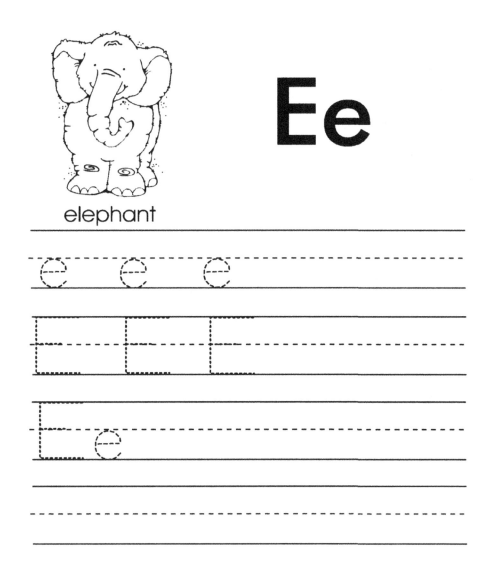

elephant

Ee

E-F Pictures

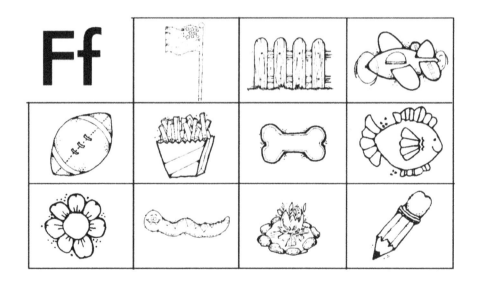

EFGH Alpha Cards

Ending Sounds

Write the ending sound of each picture.   Ending Sounds

F Worksheet Big

Ff

Cut out the pictures on the Ff page in the dotted lines and glue all the pictures that start with the Ff sound on the fish page.

F Writing

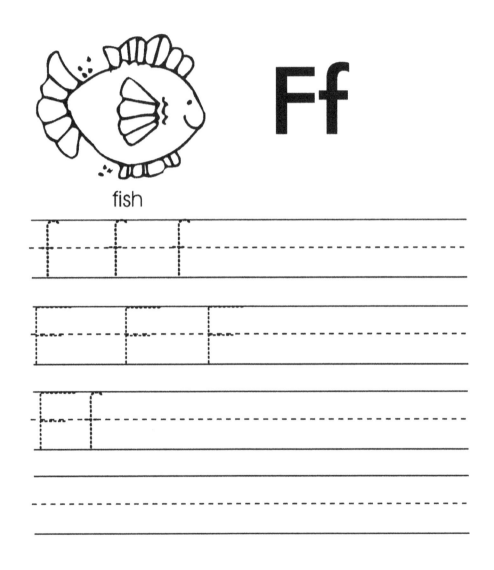

fish

Ff

G Worksheet Big

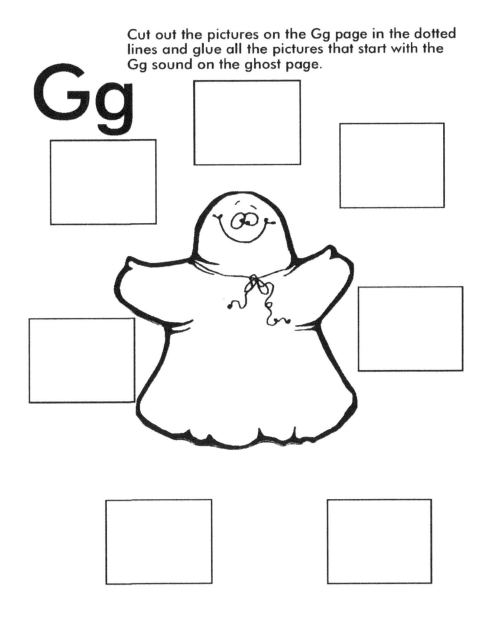

Cut out the pictures on the Gg page in the dotted lines and glue all the pictures that start with the Gg sound on the ghost page.

G Writing

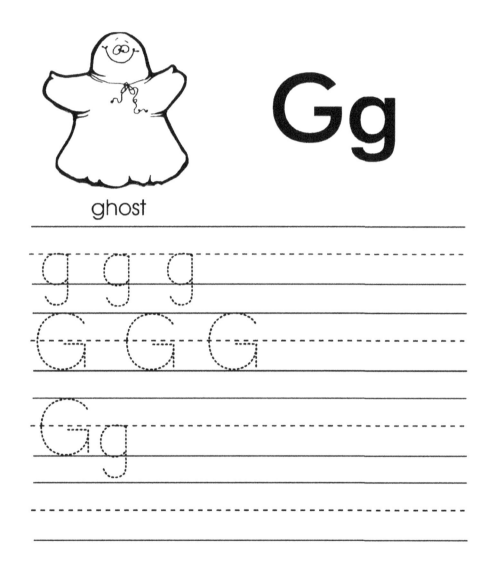

ghost

Gg

Garden Rhyming

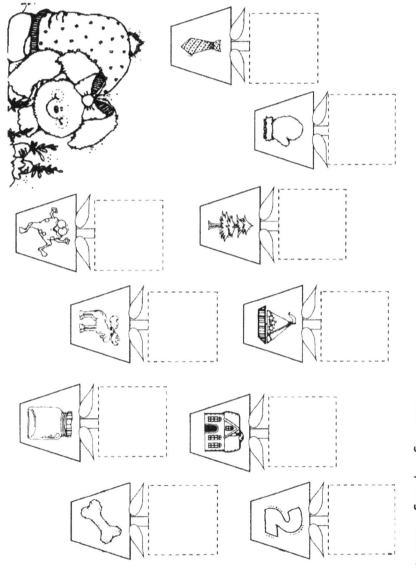

Matching Rhyming Pictures

Garden Rhyming Pictures

G-H Pictures

H Worksheet Big

Cut out the pictures on the Hh page in the dotted lines and glue all the pictures that start with the Hh sound on the hippo page.

H Writing

hippo

Hh

I Worksheet Big

I i Cut out the pictures on the Ii page in the dotted lines and glue all the pictures that start with the Ii sound on the igloo page.

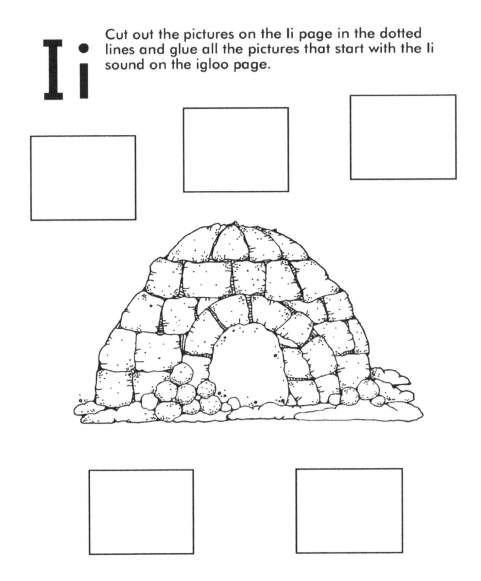

I Writing

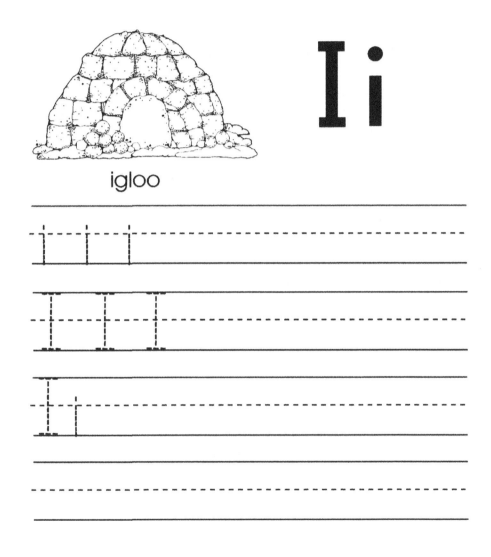

igloo

I i

I-J Pictures

I-L Alpha Cards

J Worksheet Big

Cut out the pictures on the Jj page in the dotted lines and glue all the pictures that start with the Jj sound on the jar page.

J Writing

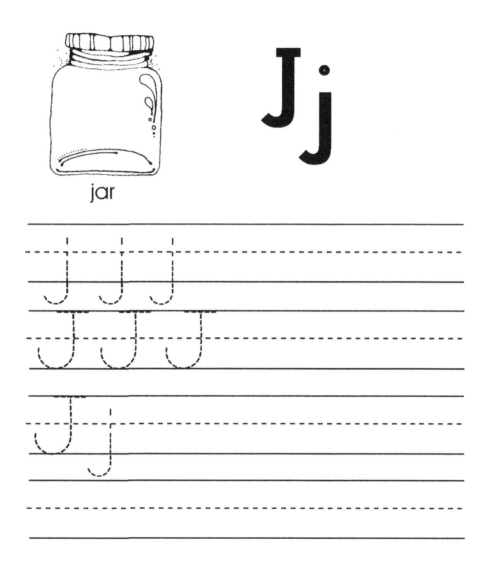

jar

J j

K Worksheet Big

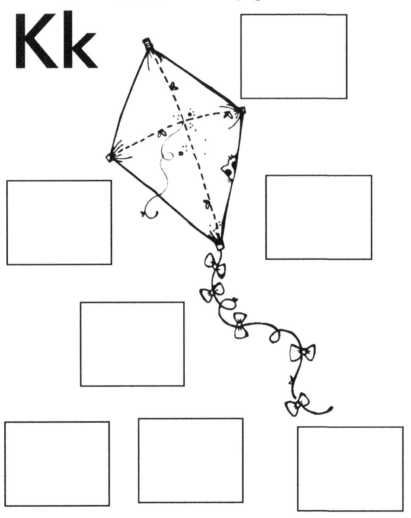

Cut out the pictures on the Kk page in the dotted lines and glue all the pictures that start with the Kk sound on the kite page.

K Writing

Cut out the pictures on the Kk page in the dotted lines and glue all the pictures that start with the Kk sound on the kite page.

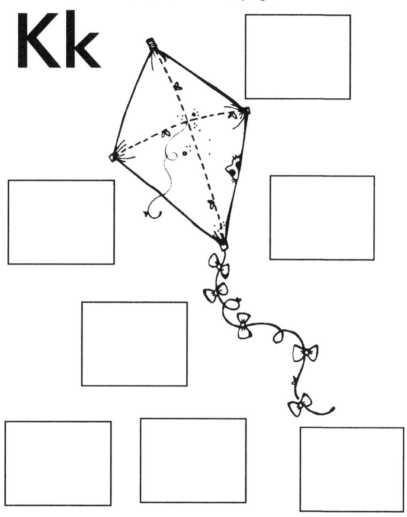

K-L Pictures

L Worksheet Big

Cut out the pictures on the Ll page in the dotted lines and glue all the pictures that start with the Ll sound on the lion page.

L Writing

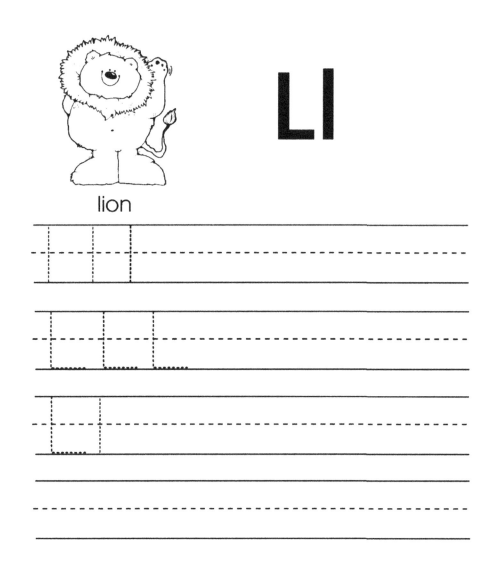

lion

Ll

M Worksheet Big

Mm

Cut out the pictures on the Mm page in the dotted lines and glue all the pictures that start with the Mm sound on the mouse page.

M Writing

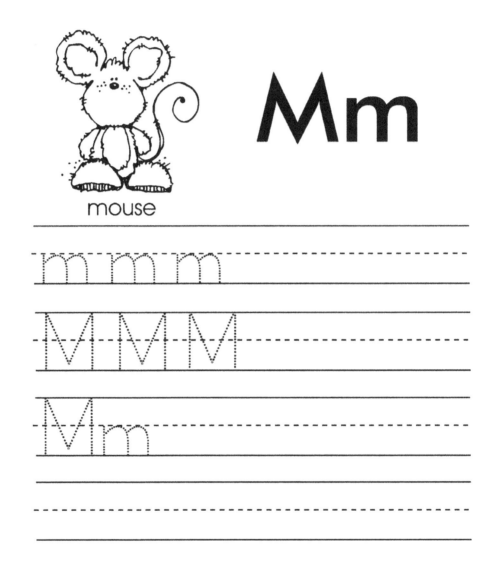

mouse

Mm

Middle A or O

Middle A or O Pictures

Middle Sounds

Middle Sounds (Ee or Ii)

b__ll	t__n	p__g
ch__ck	p__n	h__n
f__sh	b__d	qu__lt
sl__d	sh__ll	m__tt

M-N Pictures

M-P Alpha Cards

N Worksheet Big

Nn

Cut out the pictures on the Nn page in the dotted lines and glue all the pictures that start with the Nn sound on the nest page.

N Worksheet Big

nest

Nn

O Worksheet Big

Cut out the pictures on the Oo page in the dotted lines and glue all the pictures that start with the Oo sound on the octopus page.

O Writing

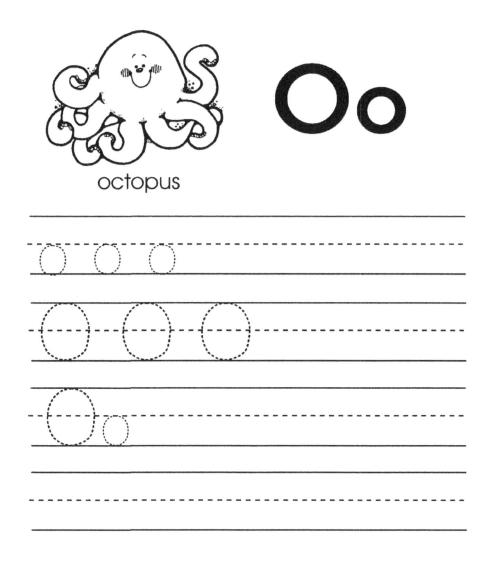

octopus

O-P Pictures

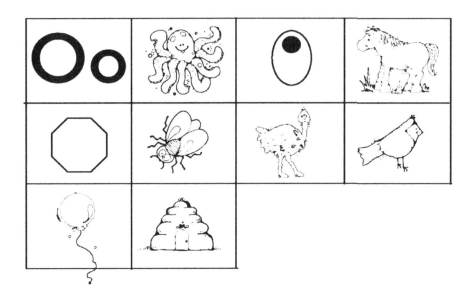

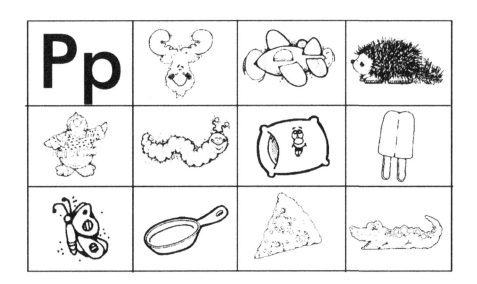

P Worksheet Big

Cut out the pictures on the Pp page in the dotted lines and glue all the pictures that start with the Pp sound on the pig page.

P Writing

pig

Pp

Q Worksheet Big

Cut out the pictures on the Qq page in the dotted lines and glue all the pictures that start with the Qq sound on the quilt page.

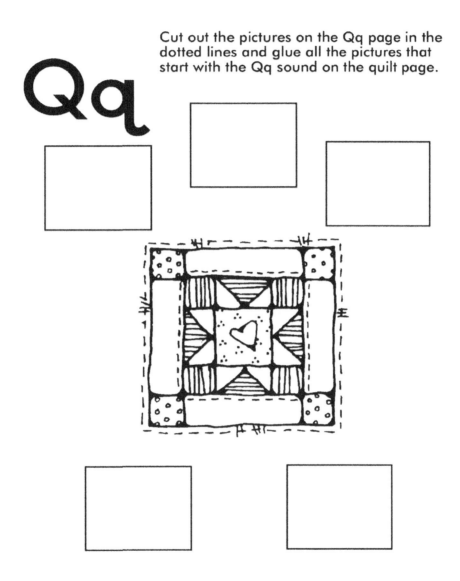

Q Writing

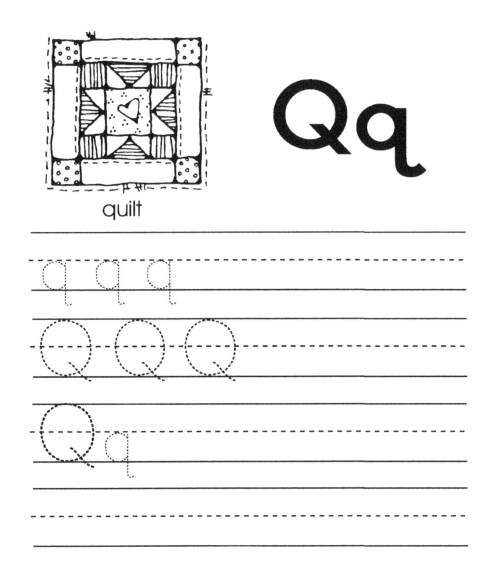

quilt

Qq

Q-R Pictures

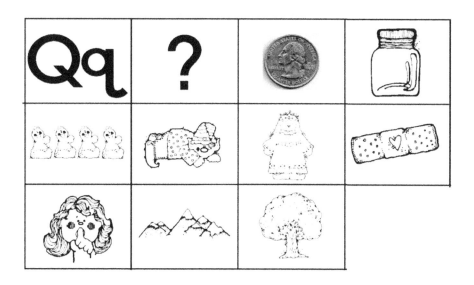

Q-T Alpha Cards

R Worksheet Big

Cut out the pictures on the Rr page in the dotted lines and glue all the pictures that start with the Rr sound on the rainbow page.

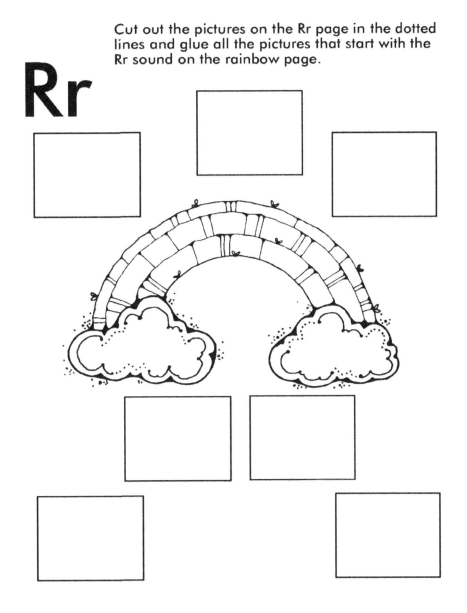

R Writing

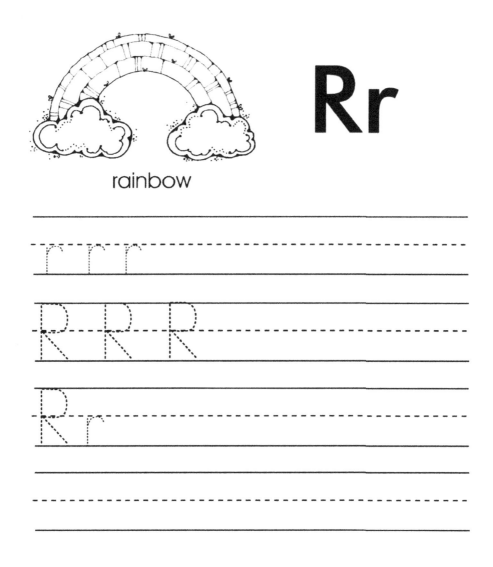

rainbow

Rr

S Worksheet Big

Cut out the pictures on the Ss page in the dotted lines and glue all the pictures that start with the Ss sound on the sun page.

S Writing

sun

Ss

S-T Pictures

Short Vowels

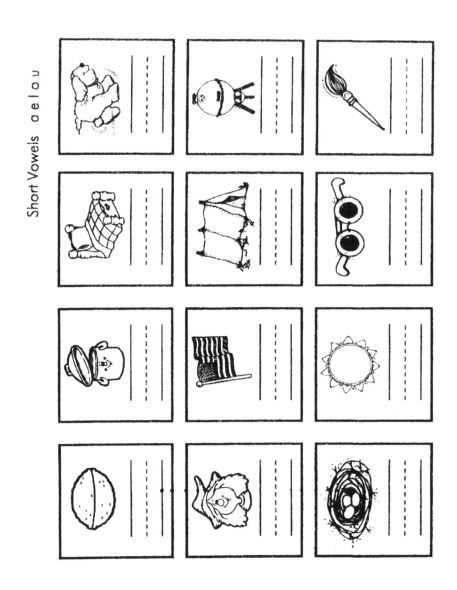

Sight Words

where	yes
this	me
is	for
no	go
it	my

Sight Words

what	look
have	can
do	to
is	the
she	not

Sight Words

are	and
at	we
you	see
he	I
here	has

Sight Words

too	good
said	big
up	home
like	was
have	from

Sight Words

too	good
said	big
up	home
like	was
have	from

Sight Words

ten	blue
orange	purple
yellow	green
red	

Small Alphabet

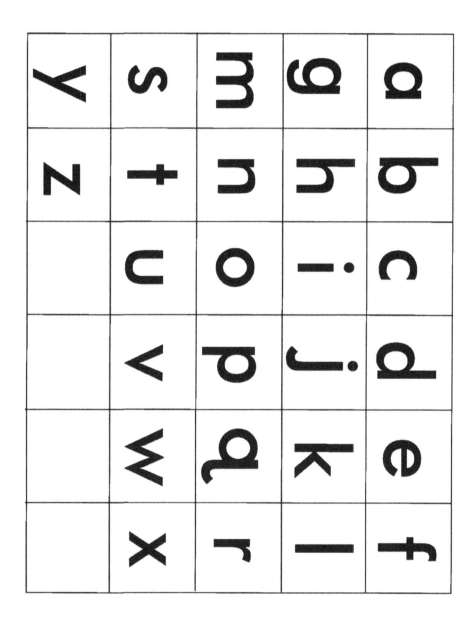

T Worksheet Big

Cut out the pictures on the Tt page in the dotted lines and glue all the pictures that start with the Tt sound on the turkey page.

T Writing

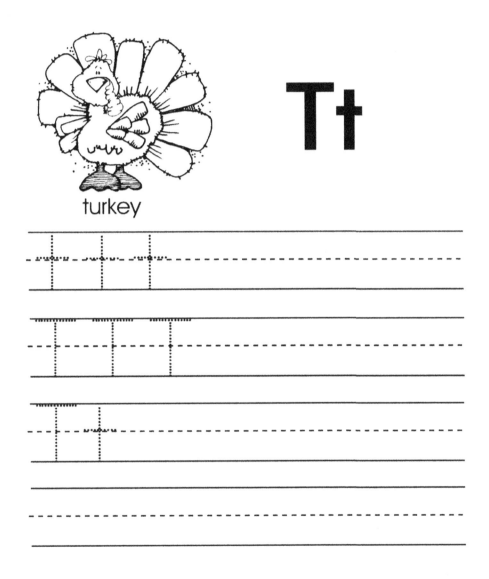

turkey

Tt

U-V Pictures

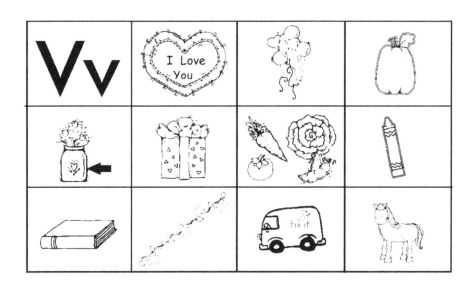

U Worksheet Big

Cut out the pictures on the Uu page in the dotted lines and glue all the pictures that start with the Uu sound on the umbrella page.

U Writing

umbrella

Uu

UVWX Alpha Cards

V Worksheet Big

Cut out the pictures on the Vv page in the dotted lines and glue all the pictures that start with the Vv sound on the van page.

V Writing

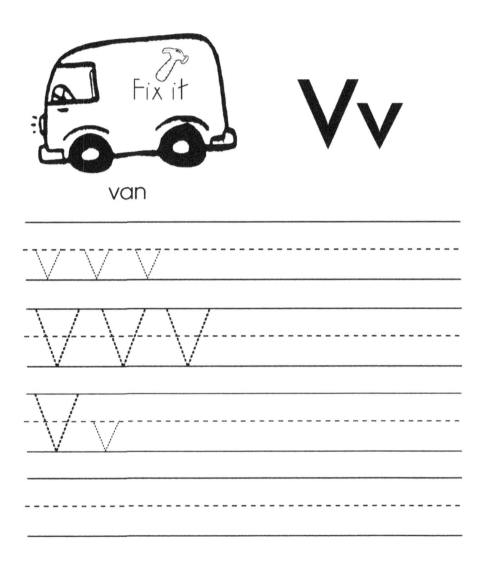

van

Vv

W Worksheet Big

Ww

Cut out the pictures on the Ww page in the dotted lines and glue all the pictures that start with the Ww sound on the wagon page.

W Writing

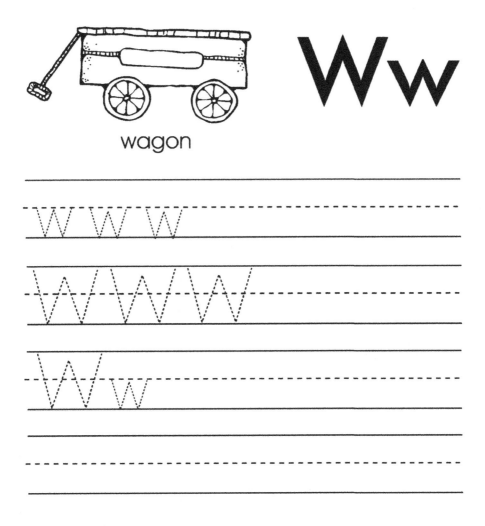

wagon

W w

W-Y Pictures

X Writing

xray

Xx

Y Worksheet Big

Cut out the pictures on the Yy page in the dotted lines and glue all the pictures that start with the Yy sound on the yarn page.

Y Writing

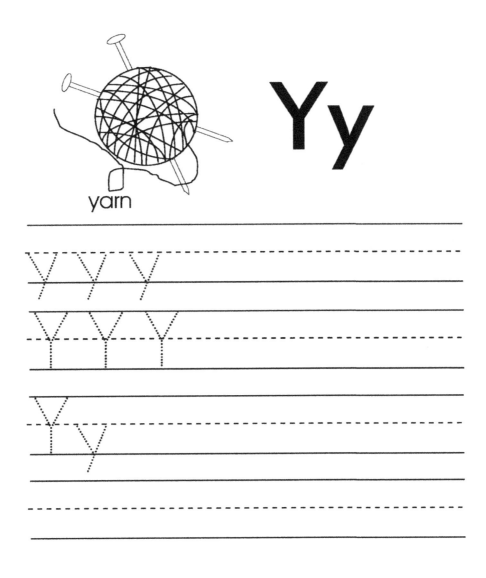

yarn

Yy

Y-Z Alpha Cards

Z Pictures

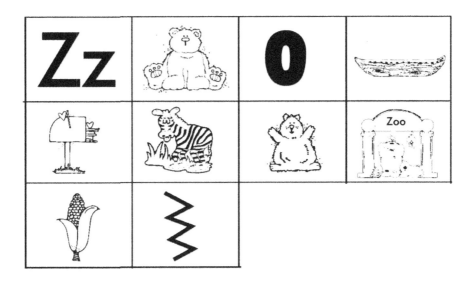

Z Worksheet Big

Cut out the pictures on the Zz page in the dotted lines and glue all the pictures that start with the Zz sound on the zebra page.

Z Writing

zebra

Zz

Made in the USA
Las Vegas, NV
02 November 2023

80122677R00070